Urban Animals

Isabel Hill

Star Bright Books
New York

To my daughter, Anna, whose keen observation and love of animals inspired me to look for, and photograph, urban animals.

Special thanks to my editor, Rena D. Grossman, for her imaginative ideas, collaborative sensibility, and constant encouragement.

-I.H.

Published in the United States of America by Star Bright Books, Inc., 30-19 48th Avenue, Long Island City, NY 11101.

The name Star Bright Books and the Star Bright Books logo are registered trademarks of Star Bright Books, Inc. Please visit www.starbrightbooks.com. For bulk orders, please email orders@starbrightbooks.com

Illustrations and design by Andrea Erekson.

Hardback ISBN-13: 978-1-59572-209-6
Paperback ISBN-13: 978-1-59572-210-2

Printed in Canada   9 8 7 6 5 4 3 2 1

Library of Congress Cataloging-in-Publication Data

Hill, Isabel (Isabel T.)
 Urban animals / Isabel Hill.
    p. cm.
 ISBN 978-1-59572-209-6 (hardback : alk. paper) -- ISBN 978-1-59572-210-2 (pbk. : alk. paper)
 1. Decoration and ornament, Architectural--Juvenile literature. 2. Architecture--Details--Juvenile literature. 3. Animal sculpture--Juvenile literature. I. Title.
 NA2840.H56 2009
 729--dc22
                                    2009028378

Come to the city and you will find,
animals, animals of every kind.

Walking the streets is like visiting a zoo,
but the animals are on buildings, so come find a few.

There are so many directions you can take.

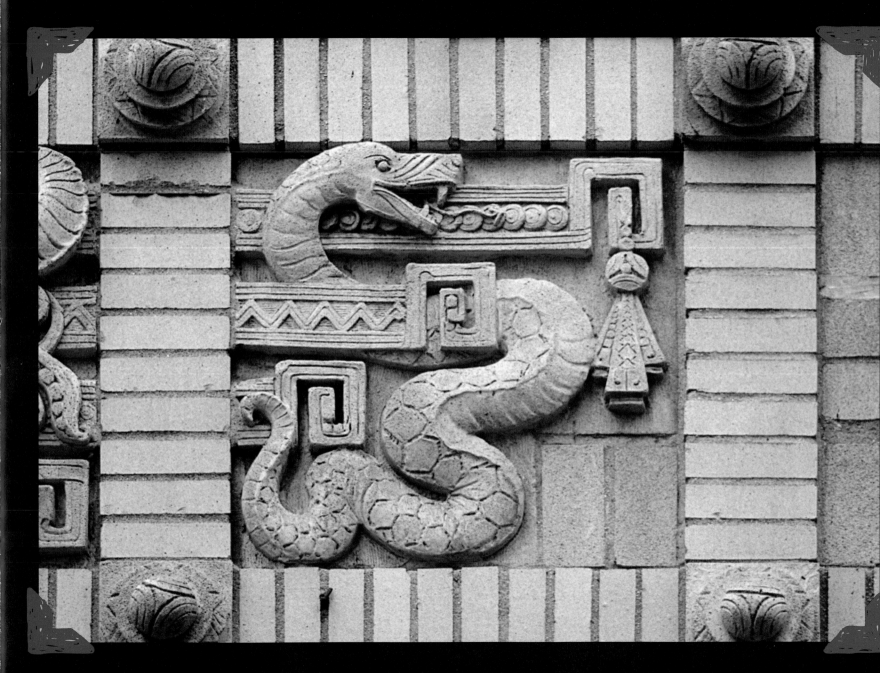

but watch where you're going because there's a snake.

In this keyStone with its tail in a curl,

sits a busy city squirrel.

The details of this column have lasted for years.

you can still see a dog with long droopy ears.

Over an entrance they shimmer and glow,

This animal roars and makes a loud racket.

a lion is used as a building bracket.

Now take a look at this building's face,

the tortoise and hare are running a race.

Protecting a window with grace and skill,

Reminding us milk was once bottled inside,

below stone dentils cows still reside.

They circle the building but never land,

these geese fly homeward in a wide bronze band.

Guarding his stoop, alert and stout,

a boar reveals big teeth and a snout.

This Broadway theater is one of a kind,

with a bunny peering out from the cornice line.

Each supporting its own flagpole,

these elephants play an important role.

Resting in an architectural panel,

two fish swim in neither sea nor channel.

A belt course divides two of these floors,

and an owl perches above each side of the door.

Look at this stable and find the medallion.

is the horse you See a mare or a stallion?

A shell, a flower, a twig, a leaf,

a songbird nestles in a stone relief.

A skyscraper reaches up to the sky,

and an alligator climbs 28 stories high.

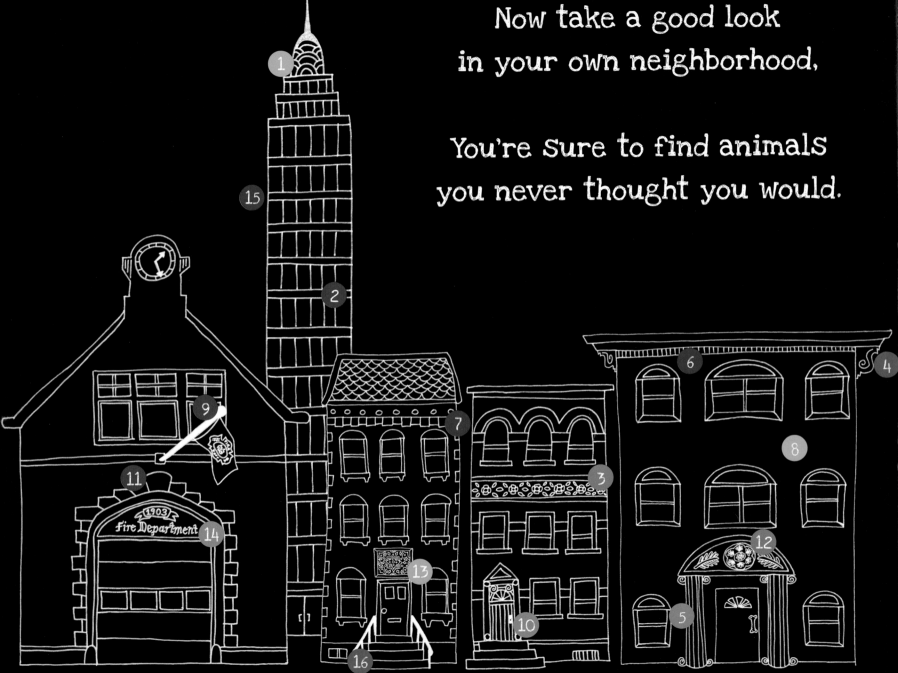

Now take a good look
in your own neighborhood,

You're sure to find animals
you never thought you would.

Architectural Glossary

1 Art Deco: A style of architecture that uses simple, bold geometric shapes, such as circles, squares, rectangles, and ovals.

2 Band: A flat, horizontal strip of stone or metal that splits a building into sections.

3 Belt Course: A thin, horizontal band of stone, brick, or tile that goes across the front of a building like a belt.

4 Bracket: A simple upside down "L" shaped structure that supports a part of a building.

5 Column: An upright structure, usually in the shape of a cylinder, that supports a part of a building.

6 Cornice: The top section of a building where the wall meets the roof.

7 Dentils: Small, teeth-like square blocks.

8 Face: The outside wall of a building.

9 Flagpole: A stick that holds a flag.

10 Grille: A decorative frame of metal bars that protects a door or window.

11 Keystone: A wedge-shaped stone in the middle of an arch.

12 Medallion: A circle or oval that looks like a medal.

13 Panel: A frame, usually in the shape of a rectangle, that is raised or set back.

14 Relief: Sculpture or carving that extends out from a flat surface of a building.

15 Skyscraper: A very tall building.

16 Stoop: An area with a platform and steps leading to the entrance of a building.

Animal Habitats

B. W. Mayer Building
130 East 25th St., Manhattan
Built: 1916
Architect: Herman Lee Meader

Kings County Savings Bank
135 Broadway, Brooklyn
Built: 1868
Architects: King & Wilcox

162 West 84th St., Manhattan
Built: 1891
Architect: Edward Wenz

Maritime Exchange Building
80 Broad St., Manhattan
Built: 1930
Architects: Sloan & Robertson

88 Prospect Park West, Brooklyn
Built: 1908-09
Owner/Architect: Roundtree Realty Co.

1040 Park Ave., Manhattan
Built: 1924
Architects: Delano & Aldrich

Central Savings Bank
2100-2108 Broadway, Manhattan
Built: 1927-28
Architects: York & Sawyer
Ironwork: Samuel Yellin

Sheffield Farms Milk Plant
1368 Fulton St., Brooklyn
Built: 1915
Architect: Frank A. Rooke

Chanin Building
122 East 42nd St./125 East 41st St., Manhattan
Built: 1927-29
Architect: Sloan & Robertson with
Rene Chamberllan & Jacques L. Delamarre

250 Garfield Place, Brooklyn
Built: 1891
Architect: Helmer Westoen

Bunny Theater
3589 Broadway, Manhattan
Built: 1913
Architect: George H. Pelham

Belmont Plaza Hotel
541 Lexington Ave., Manhattan
Built: 1928
Architect: Emery Roth

568 Fourth St., Brooklyn
Built: 1909
Architect: Arthur R. Koch

210 East 73rd St., Manhattan
Built: 1928-1931
Architect: Emery Roth

George S. Bowdoin Stable
149 East 38th St., Manhattan
Built: 1902
Architect: Ralph S. Townsend

46 West 90th St., Manhattan
Built: 1901-02
Architect: Theodore E. Thomson

Liberty Tower
55 Liberty St., Manhattan
Built: 1909-10
Architect: Henry Ives Cobb